BOOK REVIEWS THAT SELL

Discover the Secrets of Getting a Boatload of Great Reviews

Dr. Gary Webb

PublishingPoints

Author Services

Dalton, Georgia

Disclaimer

This book is designed to provide information on getting quality book reviews only. This information is provided and sold with the knowledge that the publisher and author do not offer any legal or other professional advice. In the case of a need for any such expertise consult with the appropriate professional. This book does not contain all information available on the subject. This book has not been created to be specific to any individual's or organizations' situation or needs. Every effort has been made to make this book as accurate as possible. However, there may be typographical and or content errors.

Therefore, this book should serve only as a general guide and not as the ultimate source of subject information. This book contains information that might be dated and is intended only to educate and entertain. The author and publisher shall have no liability or responsibility to any person or entity regarding any loss or damage incurred, or alleged to have incurred, directly or indirectly, by the information contained in this book. You hereby agree to be bound by this disclaimer or you may return this book within the guarantee time period for a full refund.

In the interest of full disclosure, this book contains affiliate links that might pay the author or publisher a commission upon any purchase from the company. While the author and publisher take no responsibility for the business practices of these companies and or the performance of any product or service, the author or publisher has used the product or service and makes a recommendation in good faith based on that experience.

Table of Contents

Introduction

Let me begin with a confession. **Until now, I have neglected the importance of reviews in my book marketing strategies.** Oh, I made sure that I had plenty of reviews to get approved for various promotion websites when I launch a new book. Usually, that is about ten reviews with an four-star average rating. Mission accomplished! Case closed! No more effort to get reviews!

Then, I began to recognize more about the need for more and better reviews. It began when I noticed that most of my "competitors" have more reviews than I do. I discovered that when I saw the KDSpy[1] top 20 listing for my last book. Look below at the screenshot of what I was seeing. Notice that many of the books had more reviews than I did, even though my books were in the #1, #5, and #6 positions. 6 positions. One book often jumped above me for the #1 place, Steve Scott's *Writing Habit Mastery*. Look at the difference between the number of reviews he had versus the number my book had. His had over eight times as many reviews. But that is only part of the story. My book had only been on Amazon for about six weeks. Steve's was released on December 26, 2013 -- over two years ago. Even though my projected income is larger than his, I had to admit that over time, his book will make much more. His has staying power!

#	Kindle Book Title	More	Page(s)	Price	Est. Sales	Monthly Rev.	Reviews
1	Prepare! Publish! Promote! Book 3: Promotin...	I | S | C	215	$2.99	50	$ 150	22
2	Writing Habit Mastery - How to Write 2,000 W...	I | S | C	102	$2.99	15	$ 45	172
3	CreateSpace and Kindle Self Publishing Matri...	I | S | C	140	$2.99	15	$ 45	59
4	You Can... Write Your Book In A Weekend: s...	I | S | C	152	$0.99	4	$ 4	10
5	PREPARE! PUBLISH! PROMOTE! Book 2: P...	I | S | C	90	$2.99	4	$ 12	22
6	PREPARE! PUBLISH! PROMOTE! Book 1: P...	I | S | C	100	$2.99	4	$ 12	29
7	A Personal Mission Statement: Your Road M...	I | S | C	54	$1	4	$ 4	21
8	eBook Publishing: Part 1 - Kindle, iBook, Noo...	I | S | C	120	$2.99	4	$ 12	4
9	How to Write a 10,000 Word Nonfiction Book ...	I | S | C	122	$0.99	2	$ 2	11
10	77 Ways to Find New Readers for Your Self ...	I | S | C	77	$2.99	2	$ 6	78
11	The eBook Creation Process: A Proven Syste...	I | S | C	104	$2.99	2	$ 6	43
12	7 Easy Steps to Write Your Book: How to Get...	I | S | C	172	$9.99	2	$ 20	41
13	Write Right from God: You, Words, Writing A...	I | S | C	352	$3.99	2	$ 8	4
14	Kindle Publishing: Part 2 - Marketing and Pro...	I | S | C	117	$2.99	2	$ 6	4
15	The Art Of Book Marketing: Increase Your Bo...	I | S | C	174	$2.99	2	$ 6	80
16	Book Writing Bible: Expert Secrets on How to...	I | S | C	320	$0.99	2	$ 2	0
17	How To Write A Book: Overcome Writer's Blo...	I | S | C	59	$3.97	2	$ 8	35
18	Quit Talking, Start Writing! The Procrastinator...	I | S | C	103	$2.99	2	$ 6	6
19	The CrowdFunding Guide for Authors & Writers	I | S | C	96	$5.99	2	$ 12	42
20	How to Turn Your Kindle Book into a Video C...	I | S | C	74	$2.99	0	$ 0	0

There are many ingredients of long-term success for a self-published book. Prolific authors who establish a brand and produce lots of helpful books generally have enduring sales success. Those with professionally designed covers, well-chosen keywords, and good editing tend to retain strong sales ranking. **However, there's another factor that these time-tested books have in common. All of them have high star ratings and high volume for their reviews. All of them have plenty of well-written reviews that help convince curious shoppers to become committed buyers.**

Having seen where I have gone wrong, beginning with this book, I am implementing a different strategy and system for getting more and better reviews -- literally getting boatloads of great reviews!

This is the first book where that will be different. I have implemented everything I've learned from reading over a dozen books about reviews, nearly one hundred blog articles, and have asked several bestselling authors to get some quick insights into how they do it.

For those who only read a few pages of the books they buy, let me give you a one sentence summary of this book:

STOP STRUGGLING TO COLLECT REVIEWS. START SEEKING TO CONNECT WITH REVIEWERS.

In the following pages, it is my intent to teach you how to navigate the treacherous waters of Amazon's Terms of Service and Customer Reviews Submission Guidelines while also getter more and better book reviews. Believe me; that is an ambitious project.

Chapter 1
Are Reviews Worth the Trouble?

If you are going to sell books online, you should expect to hear a lot about reviews. That is because book reviews build "social proof." Bottom line, that means people often make decisions by looking at what other people are already doing.

All the major publishers believe in the power of reviews. That's why they send out advance review copies (ARCs) to potential reviewers to build enthusiasm among book shoppers. That's why they court the famous reviewers in large news outlets like the *New York Times*. It is why they include excerpts from reviews in much of their printed advertising copy. Reviews are part of their strategy to sell more books.

In this book, I will be using Amazon, the world's largest book retailer, as the primary example of how book publishers, book marketing services, and review sites seek to control the use of reviews. It is a vital element of their marketing strategy too.

When you visit an Amazon book details page (the page featuring a single book), you'll notice that each one has a summary of reviews just below the author's name. That prominent position reveals how important Amazon believes reviews are.

The image below is from Amazon's book page for my most recent book on the day after its release. Notice that it already had 15 reviews showing with a five-star average rating. On that day, the book had already reached 1 in its category. Yeah!

Prepare! Publish! Promote! Book 3: Promoting Books for Growing Sales (Prepare Publish Promote) Kindle Edition
by Dr. Gary Webb (Author)

☆☆☆☆☆ ▾ 15 customer reviews

The way Amazon focuses us on this review information should give us a clue about how important they believe reviews are for sales. Many customers simply look at the number of stars and how many reviews have been written to evaluate the quality of the book. Others won't buy a book if it has less than four stars. If book buyers are considering buying two books, the numbers alone might motivate them to buy or not.

My conclusion? Book reviews are a lot of trouble, but they are worth it. I must confess; I have personally neglected getting large numbers of book reviews after I have successfully launched a book. That is going to change, beginning with this book. I have researched the subject and talked with successful authors to be sure that I didn't misunderstand their strategies for getting reviews. This book is a blueprint for more and better reviews in the coming year.

False Ideas about Reviews

Reviews work! They sell books! That's beyond question, but we should under-stand the reason. That will help us get the most helpful reviews possible. It is also important to recognize that various online retailers have strict requirements for reviews posted on their sites.[2] These policies make it more difficult to submit fake reviews.

Without those standards, readers will lose so much respect for the review system that they will no longer be helpful.

There are some common misunderstandings and myths about how reviews work. I want to dispel those quickly. Here are some of those crazy ideas:

1. Book reviews make very little difference in book sales. Wrong. Many studies have been done to evaluate the impact of product reviews, especially for books.[3]   These studies conclude that customer reviews form a significant type of "social proof" of a product or book's value. Many readers want to know what others think of a book before they will buy it. When they see lots of well-written four and five-star reviews and read thorough comments, the buying decision becomes easier.

2. Book reviews come automatically, so you don't need to seek them out. Not true! If you are already a celebrity or famous author, you might attract a large following of reviewers. Most of us will not have that luxury. Part of your job as a self-published author will be to convince readers who have never written a review to do one for you. You will also need to help them see how helpful their review can be to others deciding whether to buy the book or not. In some cases, you may need to send a short note explaining how to prepare a good review.

3. The hard part is getting readers to promise to do a review. Once they do that, most of them will submit one. Oh, how I wish that were true!   From the experiences of several authors, less than one-fourth of those who are directly asked to submit a review will agree to do so. Of that small number, less than half will post a review. As authors, we must understand that writing a book review is a low priority for people who have a life to live. To increase the number of reviews for our books, we must accept responsibility to make the review process as easy as possible.

4. A single one-star review can totally destroy the sales of your book. Don't you believe that! First, it may simply show that not everyone liked the book. If the vast majority were four or five-star reviews, it would have little negative effect. However, if your readers disagree strongly with a review, they can "vote it down" by clicking "no" to the question, "Was this review helpful to you?" They can also leave comments showing any errors they observe in that review. As a result, the review will gradually appear lower on the list of reviews. If your book sells to a diverse audience, you can expect some negative reviews. Seldom do I see a book with more than 50 reviews unless that includes at least one or two reviews with one or two stars. According to a study of New York Times bestselling books by Cornell Researchers, even these successful books had this distribution of rankings: 9% one-star; 5% two-star; 9% three-star; 18% four-star; and 59% five-star.[4] I have several books with nothing but five-star ratings, but that isn't a cause for bragging. It just means I didn't get a broad enough cross-section of readers to show the variety of opinions they have.

5. It is a good, time-saving idea to just buy some reviews online. NEVER, I repeat, NEVER, do this! Amazon is making great efforts to crack down on this practice.   Earlier this year (2015), they brought lawsuits against companies for selling reviews.   For much longer, they have been taking down reviews from certain reviewer accounts, often much later than when first posted.   That means the author who paid for a review didn't get his or her money's worth. Authors who repeatedly violate the Amazon terms of service may also have their accounts canceled and no longer be eligible to sell on Amazon.

6. Since my book is bigger and better than others on the subject, I will get lots of wonderful reviews. Sorry, but it doesn't work that way. The size of the book does not determine how many stars a book will receive or the quality of writing in the reviews. Some of the bestselling books on Amazon have a lot of very brief reviews and a ranking of just over four stars.

7. A badly written review can never be changed. Perhaps it can be! There are two possibilities for a bad review getting changed. **First, the original reviewer can edit the review.** That seldom happens, but it can occur if you are gracious in your comments about their review. Be very careful here. A poor response may turn off more potential buyers than the original review. One reviewer pointed out some errors in my first weight loss book. I sent a comment thanking them for the input and assuring them that I had researched their suggestion and made their suggested changes. I didn't notice anything until weeks later. That review had changed and was much more positive. The star

rating had gone from one-star to four-star! Occasionally; I edit reviews if I notice an error. **Secondly, Amazon has some rules about what is acceptable for reviews.** They do occasionally remove reviews that violate those rules.

8. Reviews can increase best seller rankings on sites like Amazon. Wrong! It is true that reviews can improve sales. However, the number and quality of reviews have no direct effect on the bestseller ranking of a book. Amazon does not reveal its exact algorithm for calculating bestseller rankings, but they assure us that only book sales get included. Learn more about their process here: **http:// amzn.to/2ORDkRS.**

9. Amazon has no problem with authors doing review exchanges. Wrong again. I realize this does get a little confusing at times. However, Amazon's policy is that you cannot give anything to someone for writing a review except a free copy of the book itself. It gets a little unclear at times. When one author writes an appealing review for someone's book, it is common for that other author to write a review of something the other author has written. That may be a simple expression of gratitude for the honest and helpful review. But Amazon makes it very clear that it considers a promise of writing a review in exchange for another one is consider "compensation" for the review.[5]

10. If someone writes about my book in the review section online, I am entitled to use that review for other book promotions. Not automatically! The review is the copyrighted intellectual property of the reviewer. You can, however, use a small excerpt like you often see on the inside jackets of books. That is permissible under Fair Use statutes.[6] If the reviewer can be contacted via email, you could also ask permission to use all or part of the review.

11. It costs too much to get people to review my books. Probably not. That isn't true unless you are mailing out print versions of your books. Since most reviewers are very computer literate, sending them a digital version via email or messaging costs nothing except time. It seems like most authors send their advance copies out in pdf format. I normally contact my reviewers to find out what format they prefer. I have sent mine as PDF, Mobi, and ePub. I never send a doc or docx file, however. Before sending any review copies, I set up a book pre-order on Amazon. That allows me to include a review link inside the book. I'll show you how to do that later. It also allows early reviews to be posted on Goodreads – even before the book is released.

12. The number of reviews and stars is all that matters. The review content doesn't count. Don't you believe it. I have no statistics for this one, but I have both my observations and have asked several friends about the reviews they use when shopping. A review that just says, "Great book. Highly recommended," has very little weight. Why? Because the review tells absolutely nothing about the benefits readers can get from the book. It doesn't even give readers any confidence that the reviewer even read the book. Many days, I write 3-5 reviews on nonfiction books. In every case, I normally write 150-500 words because that's what I needed to say to share a good evaluation of the book and how I benefited from reading it. I hope my comments help readers decide whether to buy or not.

13. It doesn't matter where your reviews are posted as long as they are on Amazon. Not so! The Internet has made it possible for readers to see reviews from many sources, including Amazon. Even though it is the world's largest bookstore, it isn't the only site readers use to make buying decisions. Many readers check out Goodreads.com for recommendations and reviews. Others go to various review sites scattered across the web. Ironically, if you post a review on www.amazon.com, potential buyers in Great Britain might never see that review. Why? Because they have their website, www.amazon.co.uk. Australia has www.amazon.com.au. Canada has www.amazon.ca. Many other countries have their Amazon site where readers post reviews. Each of these sites reaches a different group of potential customers.

Do Book Reviews Increase Book Sales?

I believe reviews are important, or I would not have written this book. But, let's not imagine they are the key element that attracts people to find your book among the millions on Amazon. They don't even appear on the Amazon search bar. Book reviews are one of the tools to tip the balance turning a shopper into a buyer. A compelling book title, the well-known author, an eye-catching book cover, and a motivating book description usually have a greater influence on that buying decision.

⚷ The Truth on Reviews
Reviews don't attract people to your book. Only after getting to your book page will the review have its influence.

However, many studies have shown that book reviews have a powerful influence on book sales. One of the oldest principles of sales is that word of mouth is the best form of advertisement. At one time, that power was limited to hearing recommendations from a friend of family member. With the advent of television in the 1950s, that changed. TV advertisements from an unknown actor became extremely influential.

But, times have changed since the 50s. A 2013 study by BrightLocal.com revealed that 79% of consumers trust online reviews as much as personal recommendations. That same survey showed that "73% of consumers say positive customer reviews make them trust a business more (up from 58% in 2012). Only 12% of consumers said they take no notice of online reviews (down from 17% in 2012)."[7]

Book reviews are not a direct part of the algorithm for Amazon's sales ranking. However, a large number of quality reviews can increase sales that will boost your ranking. That increased ranking can cause greater visibility on Amazon. In turn, the increased visibility boosts sales even more. The spiral of increased sales will trigger more promotional activity by Amazon.

If a customer scrolls past the BUY button on the book detail page, they immediately see other books promoted as "Customers Who Bought This Item Also Bought."

How do those books get chosen to appear in that position? There is no mystery. These are the books with the greatest sales increases within the same general category as the book featured on that page. That's part of why the rich get richer! Books that are selling well attract more sales.

A long list of five-star reviews for a poor-quality book should cause alarm. Why? As you write more books, your writing should improve. If you start off with all five-star reviews for a book that doesn't deliver value to its readers, those who purchased your earlier books will have no reason to have a second look at your later books, even with five stars.

Don't worry about a few bad reviews. No single review is likely to have a significant influence on book sales. It is the overall trend that matters most. Even some of the bestselling authors have an occasional one-star review from what we call "book review trolls."

Unless you have become a famous author, you will not automatically accumulate a lot of great reviews. Even best-selling authors who are with large publishing houses need some help. Those publishers often promote their books with review journals and reviewers in major newspapers and magazines. Then, the reviewers expand their influence by posting their reviews on many online sites like Amazon or Barnes & Noble.

The truth is, getting lots of high-quality reviews is hard work, especially for independent authors. This book is written to make the work easier by giving some tips and techniques that will form a system you can use immediately for your next books.

What Matters Most? Quantity or Quality?

Amazon is the world's largest book retailer. Right now, their Kindle Store has 3,982,665 books in the catalog. No other store is like that. They have a well-researched plan for how to help readers find and purchase books that will meet their needs and bring them back again.

Look at an Amazon book details page. It is organized to sell that book. The first things you see on the page are the key influencers that affect buyers. First, you see the book title and author name.

Right after the book title and author name, Amazon has chosen to show the star rating and number of reviews for your book. These are positioned near the top because Amazon's research indicates that this information is important to those who are shopping for books.

⌐━━ The Purpose of Reviews
Reviews do not exist for the benefit of authors. They are all about the readers.

Amazon shows two factors about the reviews. Star ratings are a way to show potential buyers what reviewers consider to be the quality of the book. The number of reviews indicates how popular the book is among readers. A combination of both the stars and number of reviews will give an immediate recommendation to buy or avoid the book. But which is more influential? Quality? Quantity?

Both have an effect, but let me help you answer the question for yourself. Imagine two books. Four reviewers have rated one as five-star in quality. One hundred twenty-two reviewers have rated the other book as 4.2 stars. Which one is most impressive to you? Wouldn't you feel like the first book is a loser compared to the second? Personally, I would think that the first author probably got a few friends to write reviews with all five stars. The second book has been evaluated by a larger group. Surely more that four of them gave it a five-star rating!

Let's simplify that a little more. The average rating on Amazon is 4.5. But, if you have a book that is rated lower, but has over 100 reviews, your reviews will convert more shoppers into buyers than a five-star book with fewer reviews.

Is This Quantity or Quality?

If you have read many reviews at all, you've seen some short, almost meaningless ones that say something like, "Loved this book! Recommended." Maybe you've also seen some that actually quoted a couple of sentences from the book description. Worse yet, you look at the reviewer profile, only to discover that this reviewer has said almost the same thing about hundreds of books. I laugh about the ones who say, "Best book I've ever read," but so are the 74 other book where he wrote the same thing! Some of these terribly written reviews have five stars. That seems to contradict the words below.

When you consider the purpose of a review, the quality of the content matters a great deal. A review is intended to give readers additional, personal information about the book and its benefits. Since different people evaluate books from personal perspectives, you would expect some differences in how they rate and describe the quality of the books.

Ideally, the written content of a review should be free of spelling and grammatical errors. For that reason, I recommend to reviewers that they run the spell checker on their word processor before posting it on any website or review publisher. I want them to see how these simple errors might reflect badly on the review. Since the reviewer is doing you a favor by writing, both of you would normally want them to do a good job.

Summary and Questions

Amazon believes in the power of book reviews. Want proof? Just look at any book details page. Book review star-rankings are prominently displayed beneath the author's name. It also tells how many reviews have been posted.

The quantity and star rating of reviews is displayed more prominently on Amazon than the actual reviews. Doesn't that say something? I'm afraid that it does, but it also gives a false impression. Some people imagine that no one is reading reviews. However, the most dedicated readers are also the most likely to check out the reviews before spending their money to buy. **Quality and quantity are both important to readers searching for their next book purchase.**

Action Steps:

1) Since the quantity of reviews is important, what goals have you established for your next book launch? How many book reviews do you want to appear on the first day of your launch? How many do you want after one week? A month? A year?

2) Because the quality of reviews is also important, what steps do you plan to take to ensure that you are requesting reviews from those who will supply well-written reviews? Where will you find those reviewers? How can you predict the kind of reviews they will write for your books?

3) If you have access to KDSpy, [KDSpy is a browser extension for Chrome and Firefox. It is used to quickly view comparative data about books listed in the top 100 best-selling books in categories on Amazon. You can find out more about it at http:// bit.ly/1XmJViN.] **look inside the best category for one of your previous books.** Compare the estimated sales with the number of reviews. What is your conclusion about the affect of reviews on book sales?

Chapter 2
An Uneasy Truce
Between Authors & Amazon

Authors complain about Amazon. Is that surprising? Here is the most amazing opportunity that authors have had in the history of the world. Especially since the introduction of the Amazon Kindle ebook reader, an author is able to get a book published in record time and with minimal or no up-front cost at all. He or she can have a book distributed all around the world with the highest royalties ever paid. In addition, the Amazon platform provides tremendous resources to make the work even easier. So, why are so many authors doing all this complaining?

The single complaint that I hear most is about the Amazon review system. In particular, I hear about Amazon making it more difficult for self-published authors to get and keep reviews. In this chapter, I hope to clarify some of these issues and encourage authors to accept responsibility for getting more and better reviews. Let's tackle the biggest complaint first.

Why Does Amazon Remove So Many Reviews

In recent months, some of my friends have complained that Amazon has removed some of their reviews, usually even the best ones. To them, it seems like Amazon is just being unfair. Let me explain.

Amazon wants long-term, high-volume sales. As authors, we have tunnel vision. We look at the sales of our books instead of the bigger picture. We want Amazon to have the policies that bring us the greatest and quickest profit.

When compared with authors, Amazon is more strategic in its business planning. It is seeking to maximize book sales and profits, without regard to how any one author is doing. Reviews are an important part of that process. If people lose respect for the honesty of the review system, then Amazon's overall sales would fall.

Amazon and You

Amazon is more interested in its profits than yours. Duh!

Amazon is less concerned about your individual profits than the combined profits rolling in from thousands of authors. That's what drives their profits higher. They want their overall sales to be high. A questionable review system undermines their marketing plan.

When Amazon removes a review, it usually does not contact either the reviewer or the author to explain why that review violates their terms of service. The review just disappears, leading to speculation about why that happened. One of the most common reasons is that Amazon has determined a particular reviewer has a close relationship with the author. Some authors are frustrated because Amazon's computers have made a connection between them and their "friends" on Facebook or other social media.

Ways to Avoid Reviews Being Removed

Writing and posting fake reviews is not just against the terms of service at most review sites or publications; it is also against Federal Trade Commission truth-in-advertising laws.

In recent months and years, Amazon has been trying to be more aggressive in enforcement of its terms of service and guidelines for reviews. As a result, the number of reviews Amazon is removing has increased. Usually, these happen without any notice to either the author or to the reviewer.

For these reasons, I would like to share some thoughts about how to avoid having reviews removed. These apply to both authors and reviewers.

Avoid even the slightest appearance of a review swap. If you only write reviews for those who have written reviews for you, it doesn't look good. Maybe you follow my suggestions in a previous chapter about where to find reviewers. One of those is to identify those who have reviewed your previous books and put them on your prospective reviewers list. If I notice that they are authors, I also watch for them to release new books. When they do, I often write a review. That builds my connection with them, but if they were the only ones I contact when asking for reviews, I would be establishing a pattern that looks like a review swap. By the way, if you already did a review of an author's book months ago, they are likely to accept your invitation to do one on your new release.

Avoid paid blog tours. Blog tours are a great way to get more reviews. And to promote book sales However, if you pay the tour organizer to be included in a tour that promotes writing reviews, Amazon may consider them paid reviews even though the individual reviewer didn't receive a penny. Book marketing guru Penny Sansevieri[8] has explained this based on her contact Amazon Author Central. You might also want to get acquainted with author Amber R. Allen's blog[9] for some tips about this and other Amazon review problems.

Using identical IP addresses. If you contact all your friends at work or students on campus asking for reviews, you may get many that will later be removed because they were submitted from the same IP address (a unique series of numbers used to identify each computer when connected to the Internet). This can make it appear that one individual posted all these reviews from the same computer.

Do not write sales copy. I had one review removed because my final sentence was a call to action. I strongly urged the readers to buy the book. I didn't just give information about why I liked the book; I wrote the review with some emotion and intensity to move them to buy. At the end, I wrote a call to action -- telling the the reader to get their copy NOW! It can be a matter of discussion what counts as promotional content, but Amazon is the ultimate authority. In the case I mentioned, I removed that portion from the review, re-posted it, and it was allowed. Usually, when Amazon removes a review, they will not allow it to be replaced. As an author, you should make it a practice to read your reviews. When a review appears to violate known policies of the review site, enter a comment asking the reviewer to make the needed changes. After they fix the problem, you can edit or delete your comment.

Be very careful with gifting books through gift cards. It is less likely for Amazon to detect and remove a book if it was purchased with a traditional gift card than with their online gift system.

Avoid public interactions with other authors on social media.   Amazon removes reviews because of close relationships between the author and the reviewer.   Sometimes, the relationship is obvious when they have the same last name and address.   Sometimes, it is pretty clear because the reviewer mentions a friendship in the review. At other times, it is unclear why Amazon concluded that a relationship exists. Recently, I've read reports about Amazon doing data mining of social media to detect interactions between authors.[10]   It seems unreasonable because many authors contact one another without having any real relationship. You must be very cautious about interactions with your reviewers.   Do not use public, visible posts on social media because data mining publicly available documents is legal. Limit most of your interactions on social media to private messages.   Follow ethical principles when dealing with other authors and keep your communication professional.

The Most Common Violations of Amazon's Terms of Service

Every major review site or journal has something similar to Amazon's Terms of Service.   The reason is simple. All of them want to maintain the integrity of their review system.   If the reviews are not credible and valuable to potential readers, then why publish reviews at all?   While all review systems have such standards, enforcement is often inconsistent.   This results in complaints from authors and readers. Authors complain when favorable reviews are removed or when they are suddenly banned from selling on Amazon because of repeated violations.   Readers complain when the reviews are deceptive and misleading.   They want to be able to trust what the reviews say -- at least as an honest opinion from someone who read the book.

Amazon's Terms of Service are similar to the ones used by other review locations. If you understand them, you should not have a problem when reviews are posted on any of these sites.   Here is the best place to see Amazon's policies regarding reviews: http://amzn.to/1bfL0zO.   Let's look at some of the most common violations of these policies.

Paid reviews from Fiverr, virtual assistants, or review sites.   Actually, some websites exist for the sole purpose of selling book reviews. A persistent pattern of paying for reviews is grounds for an author being permanently banned from Amazon. Since Amazon has such a huge share of the book market, that is like a death sentence for a writing career. Amazon is so serious about this violation of their terms of service (TOS), that they have filed suit against some of the companies that are offering paid reviews.[11]

Gift cards for reviews. One Amazon discussion forum described a company that compiled and sold puzzle books. The company began offering Amazon gift cards in the amount of their book prices in exchange for reviews. Then, the company sent gift cards to reviewers, who used them to buy the puzzle books and posted reviews. When Amazon realized what was happening, they deleted all that company's book reviews. They were furious, but Amazon insisted it was a violation of their terms of service. In fact, Amazon went one step further and deleted all reviews from some reviewers and banned others.

I've never seen evidence that any author has been banned for using this practice, but I have heard rumors of it happening. Amazon would be well within their rights to do it since these authors are using these cards as payment to write reviews. Authors can distribute free advance copies of the books, but the company previously mentioned apparently wanted the reviews to have the verified purchase label above the reviews.

Offering a special discount to reviewers. Here is a technique that is much more difficult for Amazon or other online retailers to detect. What happens is that the author arranges to have reviewers download books at a special reduced price that is not advertised to the general public. This special deal would be considered a compensation by Amazon, if they were to become aware of it.

Review exchanges. I write a lot of book and product reviews. I'll admit it. I favor those who have written book reviews for me. I don't keep count, and I definitely write more than I receive. I don't require anyone to write one for me just because I've written one on their book. However, that could cause some of my reviews to be removed. To the best of my knowledge, that hasn't happened yet, but it may. Why? Because it gives the appearance of being a "review swap."

Amazon's TOS allows nothing in exchange for a review except a free copy of the book. That includes doing a review for one another. Review exchanges are considereda form of compensation by Amazon. The "payment" for writing the review is getting one written in return.

One of the problems with that is the way authors frequently contact one another asking for reviews. Since other authors know how important reviews are, they are generally more open to writing one than the general public. Plus, their reviews are usually better written. In many cases, if someone has agreed to write a review for your book, you might ask, "Do you have anything coming out soon?" Out of gratitude for having been given a review, you would like to help them out. The motive isn't to pay them for writing a review of your book. It's just gratitude. That's where it becomes a gray issue. Occasionally, Amazon will notice this and remove reviews appearing to have been part of a review exchange. I don't know a solution to that. Since it has the appearance of getting reviews by promising one in return, Amazon has legitimate grounds for removing it. There is no appeal process that will work. If anything, complaints might cause them to be stricter with you on other issues.

Self-promotion in reviews. Amazon forbids reviewers from including promotional content for their books or products with the reviews they write. They are especially strict regarding links that point outside Amazon to other sites. Authors who write reviews should never include references or links to their books when doing a review for someone else. Amazon will eventually remove the review, but repeated violations can lead to a permanent ban from selling on Amazon.

Quotation from other reviews. That should just make common sense. If someone has already said it, there's no need to repeat it. Let me warn you about this. Just yesterday, one of my friends commented that she had two identical reviews for one of her books. One of them came from a virtual assistant she had used for a review exchange (another problem with review exchanges). The content of book reviews is the property of the reviewer and cannot be used by anyone without permission.

Profanity or spiteful remarks. It seems foolish that anyone would put foul language or harsh personal attacks into a review, but it has happened. If you receive a review with these kinds of remarks included, you can report it to Amazon as a TOS violation. Then, Amazon can remove it. When writing reviews for others, always be respectful of the author and helpful in your comments, even if they are negative. Make them as suggestions for ways to improve the book. If a particular flaw doesn't lessen the value of the content, you should say so.

Multiple reviews by the same reviewer. It is only possible to write one review on a book from the same account. However, some reviewers have established multiple accounts in violation of Amazon's TOS. Having multiple accounts can get a reviewer permanently banned from holding any Amazon account because it is considered fraud. If you are an author, you would no longer be allowed to sell books through their services. Others have established accounts for all their family members. Then, they use those accounts to post multiple reviews. Although this may be slightly more difficult to recognize, Amazon has its ways! Authors, do NOT do anything remotely related to these examples. Violations can have your account canceled and a permanent ban placed on you and your books. If you suspect you are getting multiple reviews from the same person, try to contact them to inform them of this policy.

Giving additional benefits to a reviewer other than a preview copy. Amazon is becoming more severe on this issue. Trying to be creative and encouraging toward those who write reviews for them, authors invent combination schemes that violate the letter of the terms of service. One example appears in an article by Michael Hyatt, telling his seven-step bestseller launch plan. In step five, he required three commitments to be on his launch team and receive significant benefits. One of those commitments is "Write a short review on Amazon or another e-tailer site--good, bad, or ugly." Get it? He requires people to write a review in return for membership in this elite team, gaining more access to him. That is more than just getting a free advance copy in exchange for an honest review.[12]

As much as authors might struggle with the terms of service at Amazon or other review locations, they do tend toward improving the quality of reviews. Better quality reviews tend toward higher sales, at least for those authors who use procedures that comply with Amazon's requirements. Why would authors resist that? They oppose these policies because they make it harder to get reviews meeting such high standards. That is why it is so important for you to implement a system for accumulating more and better reviews.

How to Respond to a Bad Review

A good response to a bad review starts with your attitude. If you understand the truth about bad reviews, you should have no problem handling them well.

Any book will have its critics. If you have ever read John Steinbeck's *The Grapes of Wrath* you probably loved it. Steinbeck is so readable and creative. This classic novel is required reading in many literature classes. Amazon shows 1,447 four or five-star reviews out of 1,645. But, even this great book has accumulated 71 one-star reviews. Seventy-one! If you are ever feeling discouraged over some idiot's misguided one-star review of your masterpiece, I suggest you swap stories with other authors to see who has had the most ridiculous review. You may discover that your worst one is actually a prize-winning piece of literature.

A Bad Review?

It is better to have been reviewed and lost than to never be reviewed at all!

Our lesson is simple: stop crying about a few one-star reviews in the mix. Just work hard to produce your best book and then work to get it into the hands of those who will love it.

Here are some suggestions for responding to those wonderful one-star reviews that make you wonder if you should give up on writing.

1) A bad review can be a great learning experience. Sometimes a bad review will point out a problem in your book needing correction. It doesn't matter that you paid an editor to go over it with a fine-toothed comb. You may still have something wrong with the content or formatting that will cost you sales if it isn't corrected.

2) A good response from you may cause the reviewer to revise the review. Sometimes, we forget that a reviewer can edit his/her review. We can discuss that good response in a moment.

3) Even a bad review does increase the review count for your book. If you have 100 reviews, a single one-star review won't reduce your star-rating much. But it does increase the number of reviews to your credit.

4) If you have a lot of really hostile reviews, it might make your book a bestseller! I'm sure you've heard of the book *Fifty Shades of Grey*. As of today, this blockbuster bestselling book has 33,256 reviews on Amazon. The star rating is only 3.5 out of 5 stars. A full 42% of the reviews are 3-star or below. The book is controversial and is offensive to some readers. That creates some low star ratings, but it also creates buzz, with people giving a word of mouth advertisement. I wouldn't encourage you to seek negative reviews, but they don't always give a complete picture of how a book is doing with sales.

5) Increased numbers of reviews also improve the SEO for the book page. That might cause more traffic to visit the page and buy the book because it can cause the book to rank high on a Google search. This does not indicate whether the reviews are favorable or not. It simply draws traffic because of the volume of keyword repetitions on the page.

6) If the negative review requires you to make significant changes to the book, you could un-publish it, make those changes, and re-publish with the same title but a large REVISED AND EXPANDED emblem on the front.

7) You could and should always thank a negative reviewer for any suggestions that result in an improved book. Give an appreciative comment which acknowledges a mistake and mentions that the text has been revised. For an unhappy reviewer, suggest that they get a refund for the book. Depending on the tone of the review and type of negative comments, you might also be able to ask them to edit the review by letting future readers know that you did correct the problem. You could also put a note in your book description letting buyers know that the book has been revised and improved because of the wonderful suggestions made by a reviewer. This approach encourages future readers to leave a review with confidence that it will make a difference.

Some Steps to Counter the Impact of an Unfair Review

There are a few things that can be done to overrule the damage done with an unfair review.

1) Make sure that the first reviews posted for your book are very positive and well-written. How do you do that? By contacting previous reviewers who love your work. Before the book's release, provide them with an ARC (advance review copy), and get them to submit their review immediately after the book is released. By doing this, you improve the chances of having the most favorable reviews posted first. That sets the pattern for the reviews that follow it.

2) By asking friends to upvote positive reviews and downvote the negative ones. Voting means to click "Yes" or "No" to the question, "Was this review helpful to you?" Clicking "No" will move it further down on the reviews list. To upvote a review will move it higher on the reviews list. Anyone can enter a vote without having to enter a comment. If the reviewer has made factually incorrect statements about the book, it would be appropriate to call attention to it. Otherwise, it is better to leave it alone. I've seen arguments back and forth between people over their opinions on a book. That looks bad for the author.

3) Have your "street team" upvote a selected group of reviews so that they appear on the first page of your reviews. Many readers often read only the top few reviews and do not look any further. Of course, many of us understand the importance of looking beyond the positive reviews and seeing what criticisms say in the one or two-star reviews.

4) Get more reviews. Many authors only concentrate on seeking reviews immediately after their book is released. A negative review should become a trigger for making some improvements in the book itself, but it could also mean it is time to reach out to potential reviewers to increase the review count and raise your average.

Remember this. No single review will destroy the impact of your reviews if you have a steady stream of more positive ones coming.

Summary and Questions
Things to Consider

Many authors are frustrated with Amazon because they have removed so many of their best reviews. Is that the case with you? From what you've read in this chapter, you might have some idea why at least some of those reviews disappeared.

Does it help or hurt Amazon when it removes fake reviews? Why? Does it hurt them to remove reviews that an author bought on Fiverr.com? Why or why not?

What is the difference between Amazon's reasoning about reviews and the way authors think about them?

Of all the fatal mistakes that self-published authors make with Amazon reviews, one is the most common - review swaps. If you were in Amazon's shoes, why would you object to this practice? How does the review swapping practice affect the accuracy and honesty of the reviews?

Has reading this chapter changed any of your thoughts or feelings about how you normally respond to negative reviews? What is the most important thing you can do when you receive one? What are some ways that a bad review might actually benefit you?

Action Steps:

1) What would be your strategy to increase the percentage of your reviews which are from a Verified Purchase?   What benefits would you expect from having more Verified Purchase reviews compared with non-verified purchase reviews?

2) Look through your recent reviews. Pick the one you consider to be the best. Click the name of the author of that review to see their reviewer profile. Look at other reviews written by that author. What similarities do you see between different book reviews by this reviewer? Would you want this reviewer to review your next book? If so, record the reviewer's name and any information that might help you be able to communicate with him or her.

3) What are two steps you could take to make a negative review do less harm? What could you do that might cause the reviewer to change the review?

Chapter 3
What Makes an Effective Book Review?

Most authors have read some terrible book reviews and some that are so good you wish your book was that good. We probably have some different ideas about what we want to see in our reviews. **The purpose of this chapter is to examine the ingredients of an effective book review. By that, I mean a book review that converts browsers into buyers.** However, we don't want to persuade buyers to get a book that will make them upset enough to write a bad review. Reviews are a tool to help match readers with the books that will best meet their needs and interests. After all, unhappy readers are the source of terrible reviews!

Here are some tips that will strengthen the sales impact of reviews that you write for others. You might also want to share these ideas with members of your mailing list. Who knows? They might use them in their reviews of your books!

1) The Length of Review. Suggest that a good review should have at least four lines of text. Of course, we've all seen some reviews that had fifty or more lines. That would probably be overwhelming for most readers. We should educate our potential reviewers so that they understand the power they have. They can help others who are like them to find the best book for their needs. They can also help authors they enjoy to continue writing more books.

2) Outline of key points. I have included Appendix A as a more thorough tool for helping reviewers to prepare better reviews. Every review can begin with a general statement about the content of the book. But the review must include the reader's interpretation and understanding of the book's strengths and weaknesses. However, you might want to come up with a simple list of four or five questions to help your reviewers simplify their thoughts.

For a nonfiction book, a reviewer might try to answer the following questions:

- Why did you choose to buy/read this book?

- What benefits have you experienced by reading it?

- How would you describe the writer's style? Was it easy to understand? Was it specific with answers or too vague? Did it have enough examples to help you understand?

- Was the book well organized? Did the author keep you interested?

- What did you like best about the book? What did you like the least?

For a fiction book, like a novel or collection of short stories, they might try to answer some of these:

- What was the main struggle or problem faced by the characters of the book?

- What were the main characters like? How did they interact with one another?

- How well was the plot developed? Without giving away the plot, what kinds of surprises did you find in the book? Did the ending make sense?

- What was your favorite scene in the book? Who was your favorite character and why? Who was your least favorite character and why?

- What did you like the most about the book, or the least?

- What is another book that you think has a similar theme or storyline?

3) Avoid extreme comments. "This author is completely ignorant of this subject!" "What a waste of money!" "This is the most amazing book ever written!" "It was so boring, I couldn't stay asleep!" Reviews should not be insulting toward the author, nor should they exaggerate the quality of the book -- either negatively or positively.

4) Be personal about how you have benefited. A review should not be a mere factual book description. It should give a personal expression of how the book affected the reader. It should include how the book changed the beliefs, behavior, or perspective of the reader. For some nonfiction books, this might include new skills learned. For fiction readers, it could include entertainment benefits or how it provoked thought about issues that at the reader might not have personally encountered.

Strange, But Useful Tips

Insert product links inside reviews. When you write a review, Amazon does not permit including links to your own books or links to URLs outside Amazon. However, they encourage links to other products (including books) on the Amazon website. Therefore, it is possible for you to write a review of one book, but also praise another one.

Such a review can be one written by the same author, or a similar book written by another one. As an example, you could compare two books by the same author. In the reviews editor, you can insert a clickable link from one book to the other. Do not try to enter a link directly. The review editor does not allow that. However, just above the right-hand corner of the editor, Amazon has included a button that says, "Insert product link." All you need to do is to click that button and type in the URL for the other book.

When you finish and submit the review, the book's title will appear as a clickable link. Try it. This tool is an excellent way to promote a book by your favorite author while reviewing another of his books. You can promote sales for both books with one review.

Warning! Reviewers must not link to one of the books they have written! That is the kind of self-promotion Amazon does not allow for its reviews. Amazon does allow links to books by another author, however. That creates a possibility that I believe is unethical, but it does not violate the letter of Amazon's terms of service. That strategy would be to have someone else include a link to one of your books in their review of a similar book that is a bestseller. If they speak highly of the other book, but also mention yours positively, it can be helpful to both. If they belittle the other book and then mention yours, it reflects badly on you.

By the way, you can also use this approach when making a comment about a book review. The only difference is that Amazon has located the "Insert a product link" on the left side of the editor.

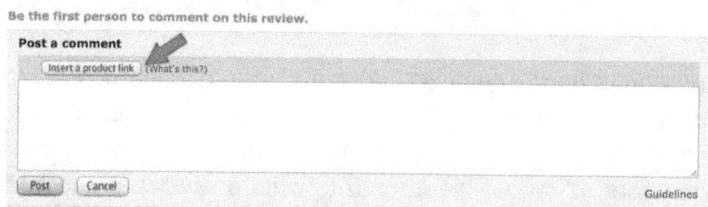

Encourage use of videos for book reviews. Producing a video review does not mean the reviewer must be visible on the video. Instead, the video can be produced using the movie feature in PowerPoint or Keynote. Much like the Explainer videos used in sales pages on the Internet, the words of the review can be placed on a slide and read into an audio file. These programs allow attaching audio files to the slides. Include images of the book cover or other relevant items along with the words on each slide. I have seen very few video book reviews, even on YouTube, but Amazon does include this feature for all kinds of product reviews, including for books.

If you would like to have some video reviews included for your books, you might need to educate some of your reviewers. You might even prepare a simple report that explains how easy it can be to prepare a video review with free tools like Jing or OpenOffice Impress. It isn't that difficult.

The process for uploading a video is an extension of the normal process of entering a text review. Look at the image below as you read these directions. Take the following steps:

1. Go to the product detail page for the book on Amazon.com.

2. Click **Write a customer review** in the Customer Reviews section.

3. Click the **Add photos/video** link beside the **submit** button.

4. Click **Preview your review** (to the left of the Add photo/video link) to make sure your review appears as intended.

5. If the review is like you want, click **Submit**.

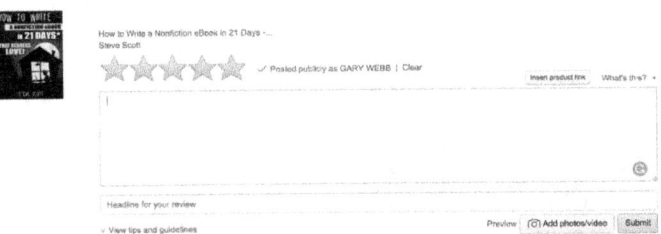

Amazon is resistant to the idea of having a call to action in a review. They believe it gives the appearance of a biased review, perhaps with the reviewer having a financial interest in the success of the book. Promotional content is another area that requires some discernment. When I enjoy a book, I often include something that is an encouragement to get the book right away. I try to avoid a call to action with wording as I might include in sales copy. In one review, it did go beyond what Amazon thought was appropriate. They removed my review without explanation. Since I always keep a copy of the reviews I write, I started checking to see what might be wrong. I immediately saw the problem. My last sentence was, "Act now. Go to the top of this page and click that orange buy button so you can begin reading and enjoying this book." I was surprised that I had written such a strong call to action in a review, but the words just flowed because I liked the book so much. I removed the offending sentence and reposted the review, almost expecting Amazon to refuse to allow another review of the book from me. I was wrong. They allowed it, and I learned my lesson. I haven't done an ending like that since.

Are Verified Purchase Reviews the Best Reviews?

I doubt that the verified purchase label means much to the average person who reads reviews. Amazon disagrees. They say, "The Amazon Verified Review label offers one more way to help gauge the quality and relevance of a product review."

But, I question that completely. I am a subscriber to Kindle Unlimited. That program allows me to borrow an unlimited amount of KDP Select books each month. If I review one of those books, it will not count as a verified purchase, even though Amazon knows I downloaded it from them. When I write reviews, I try to be helpful to both the author and the reader. So, I wonder. Is the quality and relevance of my review less than those verified purchase reviews that say little or nothing about the book's contents? I don't think so! Even Amazon seems to concede this point at times.

I've had many comments back from readers who have said my reviews were helpful, even though I got the book through Kindle Unlimited. Many of the verified reviews I've written were for books included in a free promotion. If they hadn't been, I probably would not have paid for them. If I write a review for these books, it will count as a verified purchase even though the sale price was $0.00.

Since I don't value the verified purchase label much, I would never put one of my books on a free promotion just to get that label under the reviewer's name. I would need other reasons to make that approach more attractive. Studies have shown only a small percentage of readers leave reviews, and reviewers who pay nothing are even less likely. Before I began writing books myself, I didn't write reviews when I got books for free.

Here is another reason I dislike the verified purchase label for reviews. If someone buys your book from a competing online retailer such as iTunes or Barnes and Noble, they honor your request (inside the book) to post a review on Amazon.com. Although, they paid full price for the book, it will not count as a verified purchase. The Amazon system would not have a record of its purchase in their system.

To clarify, Amazon says, "If a review isn't marked Amazon Verified Purchase, it doesn't mean that the reviewer has no experience with the product - just that we couldn't verify it had been purchased at Amazon.

"When you write a new review for an item purchased through Amazon, your review will automatically be marked as an Amazon Verified Purchase."

Verified or Unverified Reviews?

Take a look at the book detail page of one of your favorite books. Notice the reviews. Some include a couple of words, "Verified Purchase," but others don't.

☆☆☆☆☆ **Worried about launching your next book? This is the only book you need to make it successful!**

By ~~████████~~ on October 18, 2015

Format: Kindle Edition   Verified Purchase   1 of 1 people found this review helpful

Many authors misunderstand the significance of these words. I often hear someone talking about verified or unverified reviews. There is no such thing! Instead, there is a verified purchase, not a verified review.

These words simply mean Amazon can verify that the book purchase happened through them. It doesn't mean this review is more accurate or better than any other.

It is entirely possible that someone downloaded the book through an Amazon program called Kindle Unlimited. That program allows its members to download up to ten books at a time for a fee of $9.99 per month. Books obtained through Kindle Unlimited are borrowed books, not purchases. As a result, a review written on a book downloaded under Kindle Unlimited would not have the "Verified Purchase" notation. However, if that same reviewer ordered the book during a free promotion, it would be counted as a verified purchase. Why? The reviewer bought the book at the full listed price of $0.00.

A verified purchase also does not apply to books reviewed by those who receive a free advance copy. Why? The reviewer did not purchase the book through Amazon.

A book gifted through Amazon cannot count as a verified purchase either. Even though Amazon was the source of the book, the reviewer did not buy the book. However that same book, if bought with a gift card would be a verified purchase because the card could have been used to purchase another item. It was a genuine purchase.

Recently, Amazon has been removing reviews when an author uses gift cards to reimburse reviewers after their purchase. Why? Amazon considers a card given after the purchase as compensation for writing the review. If the person had not written the review, they would not have received the card, right? So, it technically is a payment for writing the review. Amazon has removed reviews when they have detected that an author has made a practice of buying several cards and giving them to his reviewers. Overall, the gift card strategy is not an approved method to get more reviews.

What About Book Endorsements?

Book reviews and endorsements have unique advantages and disadvantages.

Book endorsements are very similar to reviews, but there are some distinctions as well.

A review can be either negative or positive, but an endorsement is always positive.

Reviews and endorsements have different purposes. The purpose of a review is to give the reader information needed to make a purchasing decision. An endorsement is a deliberate attempt to persuade browsers to become buyers.

An endorsement usually does not exceed 1-3 sentences, but a review can be longer. As a result, you may need to ask for permission from a reviewer before using part of their review as an endorsement of your book. You may want this most if you can get a review from a recognized expert or a celebrity.

A much wider range of people will write reviews, often unknown to you or your readers. Endorsements usually come from someone who is a recognized authority on the subject of the book.

Reviewers are supposed to have no close relationship with the author. The reviews are intended to be unbiased information about the book. Amazon believes any significant relationship with the author may bias the reviewer's perspective on the book. However, a close business colleague may write an endorsement for your books without violating the terms of service at most review sites, including Amazon.

I have some Facebook friends who have written reviews of my books. Amazon has restricted some from reviewing my books because they have decided that it is a close relationship. Since these "friends" aren't allowed to write my customer reviews, I can use their comments as an endorsement in my editorial reviews section on Author Central. That has one advantage for them too. It means I can mention them as the author of a particular book following their endorsement! That identification is not allowed in customer reviews.

One advantage that reviews have over endorsements is that readers can compare the opinions of a wider range of reviewers who may not completely agree with one another. A disadvantage in most review platforms, such as Amazon, is that the reviewers cannot promote themselves or their books within the review. Readers can click the reviewer's name to see his or her profile and other reviews they have written, but most buyers are not familiar with that feature.

As an author, you should consider the impact of both endorsements and reviews on your book's sales. Whenever possible, try to have some endorsements, even if they are excerpts from reviews. If you do get a review from someone that you would like to use as an endorsement, please be sure to get their permission before using it. Otherwise, it would be a violation of copyright law.

How to Use Endorsements for Your Books

Whenever you ask someone for an endorsement to include on your book cover, Amazon book details page, or inside the front cover, always ask them to include their full name, title or position, and any special honors that distinguish them. This will help your potential readers to evaluate the endorsement's credibility. For example, which would you trust more to endorse a book on competitive swimming? Aaron P.? Aaron Peirsol? Or Aaron Peirsol, two-time gold medalist in 100 meter backstroke, 2004 and 2008 Olympic Games? The additional information increases the credibility of the endorsement.

For printed books, an endorsement will usually go in one of three places. It is most often on the back cover. It can be included just inside the book, even before the title page. Or, one could be put on the front cover, perhaps at the bottom.

For eBooks, it is best not to include your endorsements in the text of the book. Instead, put them into the editorial endorsements portion of your book details page. They would look something like this:

Editorial Reviews

Review

"Scott divides his steps towards change and success into four areas - Empower your thoughts, Buildi and Creating income streams form your ideas. In each region Scott offers not only sound and well-cc our new way of thinking."
-- Grady Harp, Hall of Fame & Top 100 Reviewer

"The author shares tips and tools for creating and capturing your ideas before they get away from yc the book in the first place. He brainstorms lots of possibilities for converting all those creative new id
-- Gary Webb, Author of the bestseller "You Can Be Debt Free"

"I appreciate that the book went beyond theory, and provided practical ways to implement the conce declutter your mind. Another great feature is that each section was concluded with key takeaways. T reading the entire book."
-- Rebecca Livermore, Author of the "Blogger's Quick Guide Series"

"There are some brilliant mind hacks in here that will boost your mental resilience, have you SMASH: success. The Author shows you how important a positive mental attitude is for creativity which is the
-- Ashley Black, Fiction/Nonfiction Author

Entering endorsements as editorial reviews is easy. Just take the following steps:

1. Log in to Author Central.

2. Click the **Books tab** at the top of the page.

3. Click the book and edition where you wish to add or revise an editorial review.

4. If you don't have editorial reviews yet, click **Add** to the right of **Reviews.** Along with the reviewer comment, you must also enter the author's name or the name of the source where the comment appeared.

5. If you already have at least one editorial review, then click **Edit** to make changes or add additional comments.

Sometimes, Amazon will edit something in your editorial reviews. Their edit may actually be incorrect. If you want to change it, you must click **Request a correction.** You cannot directly make these changes. Amazon will notify you when the change is complete.

When you enter endorsements into the editorial reviews, you might want to use some HTML to make it a little more attractive. Use textedit for Mac or Notepad for Windows. Amazon only allows a few codes in this section. Here they are:

Bold <b> closed with </b>
Italics <i> closed with </i>
Line breaks

You can also enter ordered and unordered lists , by using <ol> or <ul>. An ordered list is numbered, while an unordered one has bullets. At the beginning of each line, put <li> to create the new bullet or number.

An Approach for Getting Endorsements

If you develop a system for seeking book endorsements, you can refine it over time. Without a clear system, you are re-inventing the wheel each time you seek book endorsements. Here are some steps that I believe will be helpful:

1) Build a list of potential endorsers for your book category. The sky's the limit! You might already have met some of the more influential people within your niche. If you knew several million-dollar realtors, you could ask them to write endorsements for your book on how to sell a house quickly. You could ask a famous musician to give an endorsement of your book about how to start a successful band. You might contact a Hollywood celebrity, a television news commentator, a national political government. Ask yourself..

Who are some experts in your field that are well-known and that you most respect?

Who are some of the most public figures who represent this field? It could be someone who deals with the subject on television or radio. How about Dave Ramsey for your book on personal finances? What about Tony Robbins for your book on successful living? You will never know their answer until you ask!

Look at books on Amazon that are similar to yours. Look at the editorial reviews, if any. Look at the reviews to see if any familiar names show up. For that matter, why not ask the author to write an endorsement? After all, they probably have some fans who might want to read your book because of that endorsement.

If you are writing about your career field, consider asking some of your business associates, professors, or leaders in that field?

Make the list as long as possible. Then, put it into order. **Who in all the world would you most want to endorse your book?** Send them an email or a letter first. Then, work your way down that list.

2) Don't wait till the last minute. Don't expect a busy person to make your request their top priority. Give them plenty of time to read your book, decide if they want to endorse it, and to write their

endorsement. It may take them 30-90 days to work it into their schedules. (Note: If they don't get finished in time, you can add the endorsement to a second edition of the book.)

3) Be bold. If you can speak directly with your favorite expert, you might even ask them to write the foreword to the book. I'm serious! Some would prefer that to writing a couple of sentences.

4) Use your imagination. You could contact them indirectly through a mutual friend. You could send them a personal video describing your objectives for the book in two or three minutes. You could offer them an audio version of a sample chapter.

5) Do a call to action. Remember the hardest part of being a salesman is asking the customer to buy. The hardest part of asking for an endorsement is just that. ASK! Don't be vague about what you want them to do. Make it clear that you want a written endorsement. Tell them how you plan to use their endorsement. Express confidence by sharing how much you appreciate their giving your their time and support. ASK them what version of your book they would prefer. As I mentioned with my advance copies for reviews, you could offer them a Mobi, ePub, or PDF. By letting them choose between options, you are also getting some emotional buy-in.

6) Build a bridge! You will need to contact your endorser. I would suggest that you use Google to find out if they have a website where they would have contact information. If not, check Facebook or other social media. If they are on Facebook, you can send them a private message. If you think ahead enough, you can interact several times before asking for any endorsement. You can share about your book and ask for their input. Express appreciation for everything they share. Then, ASK!

7) Follow-up with the endorser. Do NOT become a bother to them. Busy people value their time. However, about one or two weeks before your personal deadline, you do need to check with them to see if you can help them in any way.

Use this time to again express your appreciation for their help.

8) Don't forget them. After they have done the endorsement, you should contact them again with a note of appreciation. You might also send them a signed copy of the printed book with their endorsement. You might even enclose another book, even one by another author you've enjoyed. Let them know that you treasure their support. Between books, you might send them some short reports related to a similar topic. This does not violate the Amazon or Goodreads terms of service. I doubt if it violates any on other review platforms.

Summary and Questions

Amazon doesn't always agree with us on what makes an effective review. Even more so, they have very different ideas about what it means to have a Verified Purchase. How important is it to you to have Verified Purchases for your reviews? Why?

Many people don't even know the basics about how to prepare a good review. That's why I have included some tips and tricks to dress one up. If authors want reviewers to give them high-quality reviews, they should begin sharing bits and pieces about review writing through emails, blogs, and social media. You'll see why in the coming chapters.

If you want to get good reviews from others, I suggest that you learn to write great ones for those who ask you. As an example, if you write a 150-word review for another author, it will set a new standard for them. If you later ask them to review one of your books, you might even remind them that you enjoyed reading and reviewing their book a few weeks back. If they happen to look there, they will see that you did a good job reviewing their book. If they agree to do one for you, it will probably be their attempt to equal your own. I know this sounds manipulative, but it isn't. It is the principle of sowing and reaping. While it isn't mechanically so, we do tend to receive according to what we have given. I try to give more to each of my reviewers than I receive from them. It is a blessing to us both.

<u>Action Steps:</u>

1) If you have a previous book published, look through those reviews. Pick out the best-written review and the worst-written review. Compare these reviews and make a list of at least three differences between them. How would you explain in a blog article or an email, what makes an effective book review?

2) If you have written a nonfiction book, list three features of your book as you might include them in a book description. Then, list three benefits that readers can experience if they buy this book. What makes the difference between a feature in a book and the benefit a reader gets from the book?

3) Choose a free promotion book from Amazon -- any short book you find interesting. Quickly read that book and write a review that tells at least one way that your life will be better because you read it. Now, at the end of that review, insert a link to another, very similar book. It can be from this author or someone else, but don't make a negative comparison. You could just say, "If you enjoyed this book, I'll bet you'd also like [link]." Submit the review, wait till it processes and look at the review to see how that link appears.

4) Look back at the part of this chapter dealing with using video book reviews. Try to edit the review that you just created. Look below the review comments and see the "Add photos/video" button. Click it to see how it allows you to link to a video. Notice that the video will need to be a file already stored on your computer.

5) What are three false ideas about how to get a Verified Purchase label on a review? How can you get a Verified Purchase without paying any money? Why doesn't a gifted book count as a Verified Purchase?

6) Identify someone who is respected within your book's niche, someone you would want to endorse your book. Do a Google search to find a website or blog where that person can be contacted. Send them an email expressing how much you appreciate their work. Then, ask if they would consider doing an endorsement for your book. Let them know that you will immediately send them a copy in their preferred format: PDF, ePub, or Mobi. Follow the plan outlined in the last section.

Chapter 4
Getting the Kind of Reviews You Want

Many authors expect reviews to appear automatically without any effort beyond writing the book. They have that idea because they believe their books offer such great value for the money. That point has some value. If the book excites its readers, more of them may be inclined to write positive reviews. Your most effective tools for getting great reviews are writing a great book, getting it properly edited and formatted, and then putting a good cover on it.

If you go to a Broadway play that is better than you expected, what happens at the end? Lots of applause! Perhaps even a standing ovation! But the applause comes after the play, not before it begins. The same is true of your book reviews. They are the applause of readers after reading your book. You earn the applause by presenting as much or more than the audience expected when they bought the book.

Here are some of the following pointers to help your book get the applause you wanted:

1) **Deliver on the promise.** Every successful book title includes a direct or implied promise about the contents. If the book doesn't include what the title promises, the reader will be disappointed. Also, your book description should clarify more specifically what you are promising to deliver to your prospective readers. Believe me: you don't want disappointed readers writing your reviews!

Getting Quality Reviews...

Don't expect repeat buyers if your reviews are five-star, but your book isn't.

2) Quality books are more likely to get quality reviews. The lack of a well-designed cover, good editing, and careful formatting can dump cold water on the enthusiasm of your readers. That is often true even when your content is awesome. Your lack of attention to these things may look like evidence you're not caring about producing a quality book.

3) Target your review requests to the kind of reviewers who will give you what you want. Readers carefully shop for the books they buy. You should be just as careful in selecting the reviewers you contact. If they have no history of writing reviews, you are shooting in the dark. If they often leave negative reviews, so you are foolish to request a review from them. Just pray that they don't write one without getting asked. If they have never written a review for a similar book, it may not be interesting to them. It would be like taking me to an Indian restaurant. Many people love it, but I don't. I will share more about how to target reviewers later. For right now, let me just say you should screen out reviewers who are in the habit of giving one-star ratings and poorly written reviews.

4) Have some trusted beta readers who will read your book after the editor, but before asking for reviews on a wider scale. These are normal readers who don't have degrees in English. They just have an interest in your subject and are willing to give you their feedback about what needs improvement in your book. This feedback isn't for public consumption like reviews. They are for the author's eyes only, and you should take them very seriously. If you don't understand one of the criticisms given, you can contact that beta reader to ask for more information. You normally don't get to do that with your reviewers.

5) When preparing for a book launch, always have some reviewers who are ready to post within a day or two of the book's release. Some reviews are called organic reviews. These reviews come from readers you have not personally contacted. They may have seen your request for a review in the back of your book and decided to write one. Or, perhaps the reader frequently reviews books. The only thing you can do to generate more of these organic reviews is to write better books to get your readers excited about what they've read.

6) Set goals for the number of books you intend to accumulate during your book launch. Goal setting will increase your control over the number and quality of reviews. In my most recent books, I've tried to get at least 10-15 reviews because that assured me of getting accepted for many of the book promotion websites. I also wanted these early reviews to be the best quality of writing I can get. For that purpose, I often reach out to other authors to ask for reviews. Why? Authors don't need me to teach them how to write a clear sentence or structure sensible paragraphs. They can write good reviews! That sets the pattern for less gifted reviewers who come later.

7) Don't blast Facebook with requests for reviews. You are likely to get some response, but it often will produce inferior results. Since you offer a free book, even the worst writers in the crowd might say, "Yes." I have tried this technique a few times, but I've never been satisfied with the reviews I've gotten. Many who requested a free review copy often failed to write a review at all. Others gave my book five stars but wrote barely readable comments. I also got some terrible one-star reviews like the one who said, "I didn't like it. Even though I learned a lot. It was a free book, but it isn't worth the price!" Fortunately, that was the first review I received for that book. I simply unpublished the book, sent it back to the editor, and had a new cover put on it before I re-published it. Not much changed, but at least I didn't have that review!

IMPORTANT NOTE: You can get a lot of reviews through unethical ways or through extravagant advertising programs. However, this book is geared toward getting both quantity and quality. Getting a greater quantity of reviews means reaching a larger audience who will accept your offer to write a review. Getting a greater quality of reviews means targeting only those you have reason to believe would enjoy and benefit from your book AND who have demonstrated that they know how to write superior reviews. In the second case, I am also seeking reviewers who are generous in their praise for books within my niche.

Conclusion

In this short read, I have covered many of the most controversial issues related to getting reviews that sites like Amazon will accept. More importantly, I've discussed how you as an independent or self-published author can get more and better reviews. The publishing industry is changing rapidly. However, reviews will continue to be one of the keys to successful sales. Social proof will remain one of the most influential factors in purchasing decisions.

If you have questions about any of the content provided in this book, or if you have suggestions that might benefit your fellow authors, please let me know. I anticipate doing updates of the book for at least one year – probably longer. I also intend to produce other topical books like this one to help with specific elements of the authoring and publishing process. The next will feature *Book Descriptions That Sell.* I've written well over 100 book descriptions in the past year, so I've had great opportunities to interact with other authors about this aspect of book marketing. Additional topics will include formatting, book covers, categories and keywords, and others. If you have particular needs that you would like to have addressed in this series, I will welcome your suggestions and give you some advance information even before the book is released. Email me at gary@mgwebb.net

Appendix A

How to Write a Positive Online Review

Most of your readers have never written a book review. Some have never even read one. Since they agreed to do the review, they are positively inclined toward you. That is a great advantage you have by choosing those you ask to review your book. Now, help them to follow through. Develop a listing of your own that fits the kinds of books you write. Give a copy to your reviewers who seem insecure about how to write a good review. Remember, you want them to write the kind of review that helps your book succeed.

Some pointers about writing nonfiction reviews will also apply to fiction. However, I have tried to break them into two sections to make it easier to apply.

How to Write a Nonfiction Review

1. At least do a speed read of the book. You don't have to do a thorough analysis of every sentence. Just be sure you follow what the author is doing and the quality of craftsmanship involved.

2. Before launching into the text.

- Survey the book for first impressions.

- Check out the title and subtitle.

- Read the Amazon description.

- Skim the Table of Contents before reading the text.

- Read the Introduction, looking for a statement of purpose. This gives a basis for evaluating whether the author has achieved his/her purpose.

- Read the conclusion. Did the author include a solid summary of what he accomplished in the book?

3. Within the review include at least the following:

- Use the title or the main keyword of the book at least once within the review.

- Did the book fulfill the promise or expectation created by the title or subtitle? Were you pleasantly surprised that the book included something you didn't expect?

- State the most important thing you have learned or greatest benefit received from reading the book. Make this personal. The review is about what you got from the book, not what you think others will get.

- Be positive about a specific group of people you would recommend reading the book. Is it for beginners? Experts? Fans? Students? Children? Adults? Newly married? Hurting in a particular way? Creative people? Those with a particular hobby or interest?

- If the book has some minor weakness, it's okay to include

that as long as you make it clear that the weakness does not overwhelm the value of the book.

4. **Within the review include at least the following:**

- Be direct. Do you not recommend, recommend, or highly recommend the book?

- Explain what you like most about the book and why.

- What does the book say that you believe will be most beneficial to you?

- What are the author's credentials for writing on this subject? Experience? Education? Accomplishments? Awards? Leadership positions?

- What about the length of the book? Is it too short for its purpose? Is it deliberately brief to be a quick introduction to the subject? Do you wish it was longer? If so, why?

5. **Do not repeat the book description, but don't contradict it either.** Make the review have no more sentences than the book has chapters or other major divisions.

6. **Use correct English, including spelling and punctuation.** At least use Word's built in spelling and grammar checker. I use Ginger on a PC or Grammarian on my MacBook Pro.

7. **If the review doesn't deserve a 4 or 5 star review, you have extra work to do.** Send a note to the author, letting him/her know what you found that needs extra work. It could just be a formatting

error or grammar problems. It could be inconsistent headings, a messed up table of contents, or inaccurate content. That last one is a little hard, but it's possible to point out a problem and share a quick link to a good online source. The goal is for you to be able to give an honest 4 or 5-star review, preferably five stars! Small errors can ruin a book's future!

8. If you were given an advance copy of the book, state that at the end of the review. It could be something as simple as saying, "I was given a free copy of this book in exchange for writing a fair and honest review."

9. Final point. Looking at your review as if someone else wrote it, would this review make you more or less likely to buy the book? Is that the effect you intended?

How to Write a Fiction Review

Fiction reviews require a little more creativity in writing. You don't want to give away the plot, so just give enough to build curiosity and interest. You do NOT have to cover all these suggestions in your review.

Major Points

- What was the storyline?

- Who were the main characters?

- Were the characters realistic or believable?

- How did the main characters relate to one another in the

story?

- What problems or crises did the main characters face? What were some of their most exciting moments?

- Who was your favorite character? Why?

Your personal perspective on the story

- Could you relate to any of the characters in the story?

- Have you ever done or felt some of the things, the characters did?

Your assessment of the book

- Did you like the book?

- What was your favorite part of the book?

- If you could change something, what would it be? (If you wish you could change the ending, don't reveal it!)

Your recommendations

- What kind of reader would most enjoy this book?

- Why do you think readers would enjoy the book?

With either nonfiction or fiction reviews, it is important to give the potential reader enough information to make their purchasing decision, but not so much as to quench their thirst for more.

Appendix B

Book Review Request

Most of the time, you will be contacting your potential reviewers by email or Facebook direct message. I would like to share a copy of the email/message that I used for contacting reviewers for this book. If you don't already have a template for your book review requests, this one can be adapted to your needs.

Subject: Book Review Request
Dear XXX,
Within a couple of weeks, I will begin sending out advance review copies of my latest book, ***Book Reviews That Sell: Discover the Secrets of Getting a Boatload of Great Reviews***. Right now, I am seeking to identify 30-50 people who would be willing to give me an honest review in exchange for a copy of this book.
The book will include some of the recent issues with having reviews removed by Amazon. It will also seek to demonstrate the need for more and better reviews and to give strategies for finding high-quality reviewers. In fact, the key idea is to connection with high-quality reviewers instead of just trying to get quick reviews that are likely to be removed by Amazon. ***Book Reviews That Sell*** is the result of reading over a dozen books, hundreds of websites, and also interviewing several bestselling authors about the struggles that self-published authors have with reviews. You can read more about it on the pre-order page at http://amzn.to/1LKKeAy.
Since you have shown interest in self-publishing, I would like to ask you to consider reviewing this book. If interested, I can supply a copy in Mobi, PDF, or ePub formats. Simply let me know by replying to this email at gary@mgwebb.net.

Dr. Gary Webb
www.mgwebb.net

Notice a few features included in the email.

1) I immediately make it clear that I want to find book quality reviewers for my book. I then tell the timeframe for when the reviews will be needed.

2) I identify the name of the book and give the URL where the pre-order copy is available on Amazon. I also explain the basic content of the book and the serious effort involved in researching its content.

3) I let the reviewers know that I am only looking for a fixed number of reviewers. I also let them know that I want honest reviews, not fake ones.

4) I let them know that I am contacting them because of their previous interest in my subject area: self-publishing. It would have probably been better if I had individually stated that I had read their review of XXX book and was impressed with how thorough it was.

5) I let them know that I would be providing the advance review copy in their choice of formats.

6) I gave them a way to let me know that they are willing to read the book and review it. I had them respond by email because some of them were Facebook contacts. I wanted to get their email addresses for future communication.

Want More?

You've made your way through this book, so I assume you found some useful information along the way. At least I hope that's the case.

I am very grateful you took the time to read this book, so I wanted to share another way you can learn even more for FREE.

I've now written four books on self-publishing and have taken a new direction with this one. The other three were bestsellers through deliberately using the principles I was teaching. This is a much shorter, more specialized book designed to answer a few specific questions I've heard from those I've mentored so far.

I have established an online presence called PublishingPoints Author Services. PublishingPoints has a blog where I only occasionally post articles I believe will help authors. It has a daily newsletter sharing books, courses, and other resources that would make authors more successful. In time, I intend for it to become a way editors, cover designers, researchers, and others to offer their services to others at a moderate price.

I would like for you to **subscribe to the free PublishingPoints newsletter**. If you try it for a week or so, I think you'll find it helpful. http://bit.ly/1MhNt2z.

Leave a Review as Soon As You Finish Reading

I hope you enjoyed and benefited from this book. If so, please help others to learn more about how they can improve their approach to getting more and better book reviews. The best way is word of mouth to your friends, but another way can reach even more. If you write a simple review on Amazon, you can help hundreds or perhaps thousands of other readers to make their buying decision. Like you, they worked hard for every penny they spend on books. With the information and encouragement you provide, they can take action right away.

- You can share anything you think will be useful, but here are a few suggestions:

- Why you decided to buy or read this book?

- What did you like most about this book?

- What makes this book different from others you have read?

- Did it give you practical ways to apply the information it provides? If so, share what you are going to be doing differently because you read it.

- What kinds of readers would benefit most reading this book?

Immediately after reading the book is the best time to leave a review. You can leave one here: **http://amzn.to/1IceLid.**

Check Out Other Books by This Author

The Prepare Publish Promote Series

A series devoted to helping new nonfiction authors to reach their sales goals by having the reader in mind even before you write the first word. You will discover practical tips and techniques to ensure that your books deliver value beyond what the reader pays. You will learn how to write books targeted toward what readers are already buying. You'll gain detailed instruction in how to publish your book to the two Amazon platforms: Kindle and Createspace. Then, you will get intensely practical information about how to promote and market your books most effectively and inexpensively.

$2.99 Each

http://amzn.to/1LpoMxv

About the Author

Gary Webb has filled his life with variety and opportunities for personal growth and the enrichment of others. He is a graduate of four universities and seminaries. He retired from service in the U.S. Navy in 1996 and full-time pastoral ministry in 2013. In those roles, he has counseled with hundreds of people concerning personal finances and substance abuse, marriage and parenting, career guidance and spiritual growth. His wife Jane experienced a traumatic automobile accident in 2008, giving them tremendous life challenges that continue to this day. Ironically, he had just completed his doctorate in theology a few months before her wreck. That accident also has produced greater insight into the problems faced by so many families as they address health issues. While caring for his wife during her recovery, Gary has discovered a new way to share with others through writing. It has also become a means to connect with authors around the world. Gary enjoys walking and jogging, fishing, and learning everything he can about books and publishing. You may contact him by email at gary@mgwebb.net or his author website at http://www.mgwebb.net. You can see his Amazon author page at http://www.amazon.com/-/e/B008IJ4QPU.

Bibliography

Abbott, Allyson R. (2015-10-06) *How To Write a Simple Book Review: It's easier than you think.* Kindle Edition.

Ajisafe, Mayowa. (2015-08-18) *Goodreads Hack: How to Use the Power of Goodreads to Get Reviews for Your Book and Build Your Book Review and...* Kindle Edition.

Baggett, Bart. (2014-06-13) *How to Get 63 Authentic Amazon Reviews in 3 Days or Less: How to Market Your Book, Sell More Books on Kindle, Become a Best Seller.* Empresse Publishing. Kindle Edition.

Baker, Thomas Jerome. (2014-03-22) *Amazon Book Reviews: Fair & Unbiased.* Kindle Edition.

Baggett, Bart. (2014-10-21) *How to Get 63 Authentic Amazon Reviews in 3 Days or Less: How to Market Your Book, Sell More Books on Kindle, Become a Bestseller.* Kindle Edition.

Barton, E.T. (2014-10-13) *Get Reviews so You Can Sell More Book: 20 Good, Bad and Questionable Tips for Amazon's Review System (How to Sell More Books).* Kindle Edition.

Flogging, Buck. (2014-10-14) *Reviewperstar: 12 Tasteful Ways to Get More Book Reviews.* Archangel Ink. Kindle Edition.

Foster, Alex. (2013) *Kindle Reviews: How to Get More Reviews for Your Kindle Book.* Kindle Edition.

Graf, Rebecca. (2015-04-23) *Writing a Book Review.* Kindle

Edition.

Green, John. (2014-10-14) *Kindle Unlimited - Secret Guide to Amazon Reviews!: How to Get Tons of Amazon Reviews! Plus: Using KindleUnlimited for Profit! (Unlimited Success by John Green Book 2)* Kindle Editon.

Hall, Rayne. (2015-11-25) *Getting Book Reviews: Easy, Ethical Strategies for Authors (Writer's Craft 14).* Kindle Edition.

Hausmann, Gisela (2015-02-12). *NAKED TRUTHS About Getting Book Reviews Educ-Easy Books.* Kindle Edition.

Hitz, Shelley; Hart, Heather (2014-04-03). *How To Get Honest Reviews: 7 Proven Ways to Connect With Readers and Reviewers (Book Marketing Survival Guide Series 1)* Body and Soul Publishing. Kindle Edition.

Hitz, Shelley; Hart, Heather (2015-03-23). *The Truth about Book Reviews: 20 Book Review Myths, Debunked (Author Tips Success Series)* Body and Soul Publishing LLC. Kindle Edition.

Moore, Charles (2015-10-23). *Stars: How to Get Book Reviews.* Kindle Edition.

Peters, Richard. (2014-10-14) *Get More Book Reviews: Free, Proven and Ethical Strategies.* Kindle Edition.

Rao, Noah. (2015-10-30) *How to Write a Book Review.* Kindle Editon.

Rogers, Theo. (2014-10-15) *How to Get Good Reviews on Amazon:*

A Guide for Independent Authors & Sellers. (Kindle Edition)

Sansevieri, Penny C. (2014-10-16) *How to Get a Truckload of Reviews on Amazon.com. - Book One and Two: Get More Sales - Get More Reviews!* Kindle Edition.

Smith, Dana Lynn. (2011-07-11) *How to Get Your Book Reviewed - Sell More Books by Using Reviews, Testimonials and Endorsements for Book Promotion.* Kindle Edition.

Notes

_____

[1] KDSpy is a browser extension for Chrome and Firefox. It is used to quickly view comparative data about books listed in the top 100 best-selling books in categories on Amazon. You can find out more about it at http://bit.ly/1XmJViN.

[2] See Amazon requirements at: http://www.amazon.com/gp/community-help/customer-reviews-guidelines.

For Goodreads Guidelines: https://www.goodreads.com/review/guidelines.

[3] http://www.behind-the-enemy-lines.com/2011/08/impact-of-online-reviews-annotated.html

[4] http://buzzymag.com/5-ways-to-know-if-book-reviews-are-fake/

[5] http://www.amazon.com/gp/help/customer/display.html/ref=amb_link_47889982_2?

ie = U T F 8 & n o d e I d = 2 0 1 0 7 7 8 7 0 & p o p - up=1&pf_rd_m=ATVPDKIKX0DER&pf_rd_s=center-1&pf_rd_r=00Y2C1P0EKMWN NVQV6HZ&pf_rd_t=7001&pf_rd_p=1838506562&pf_rd_i=customer-reviews-guide-lines

[6] http://fairuse.stanford.edu/overview/fair-use/four-factors/.

More at: http://copyright.gov/fair-use/.

and http://www.bitlaw.com/copyright/fair_use.html.

[7] http://searchengineland.com/2013-study-79-of-consumers-trust-online-reviews-as-much-as-personal-recommendations-164565

[8] https://www.bookworks.com/2015/08/help-my-amazon-reviews-have-disappeared-why-now-what/

[9] http://annerallen.com/2015/11/disappearing-amazon-reviews-facts.html

[10] http://consumerist.com/2015/07/06/amazon-is-data-mining-reviewers-personal-relationships/

[11] http://abcnews.go.com/Technology/wireStory/amazon-sues-review-sellers-salvo-bogus-reviewers-34574985

[12] http://michaelhyatt.com/bestseller-launch-formula.html